In Tad's Pan

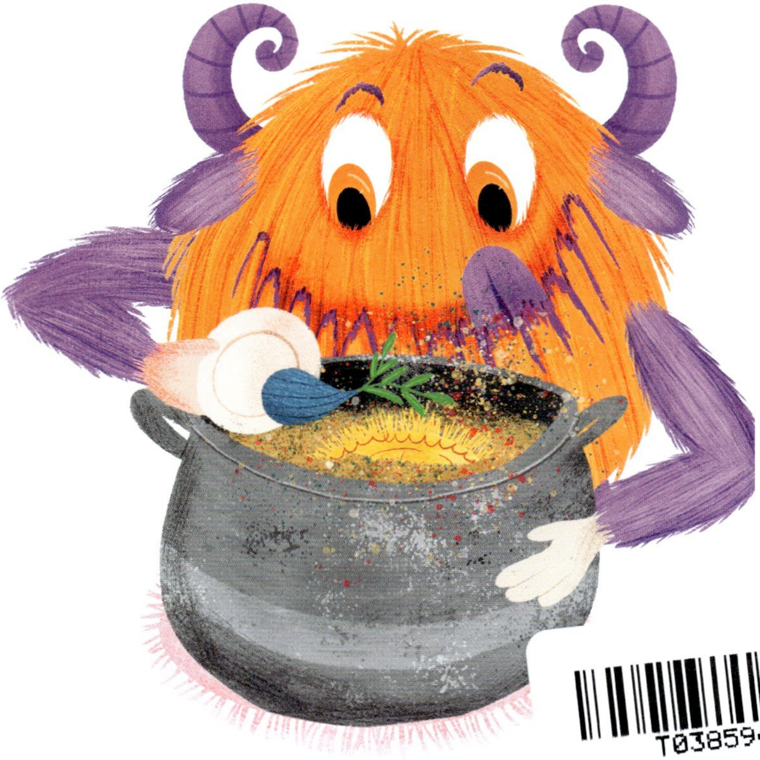

Written by Catherine Baker
Illustrated by Mel Armstrong

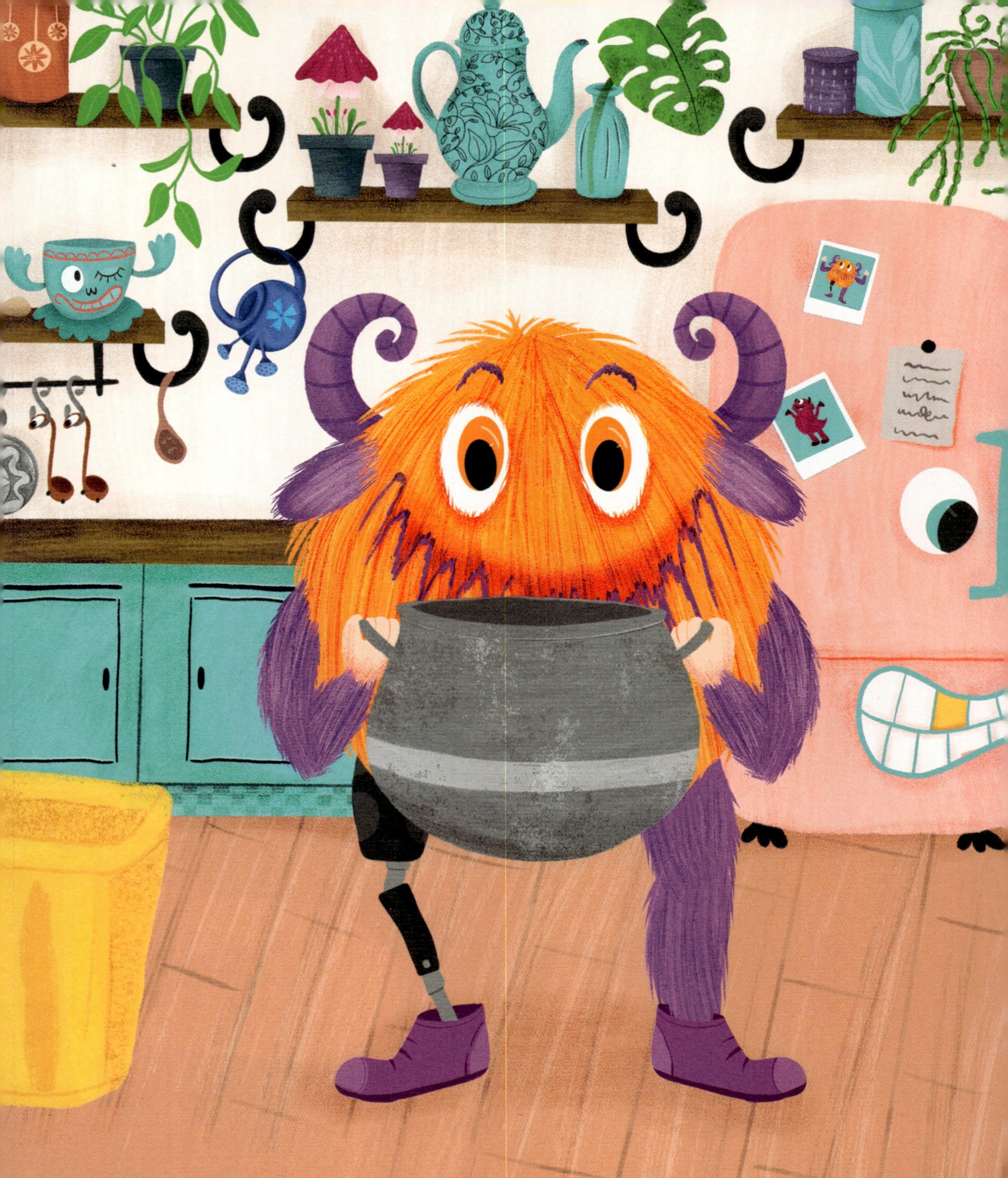

It is Tad’s pan.

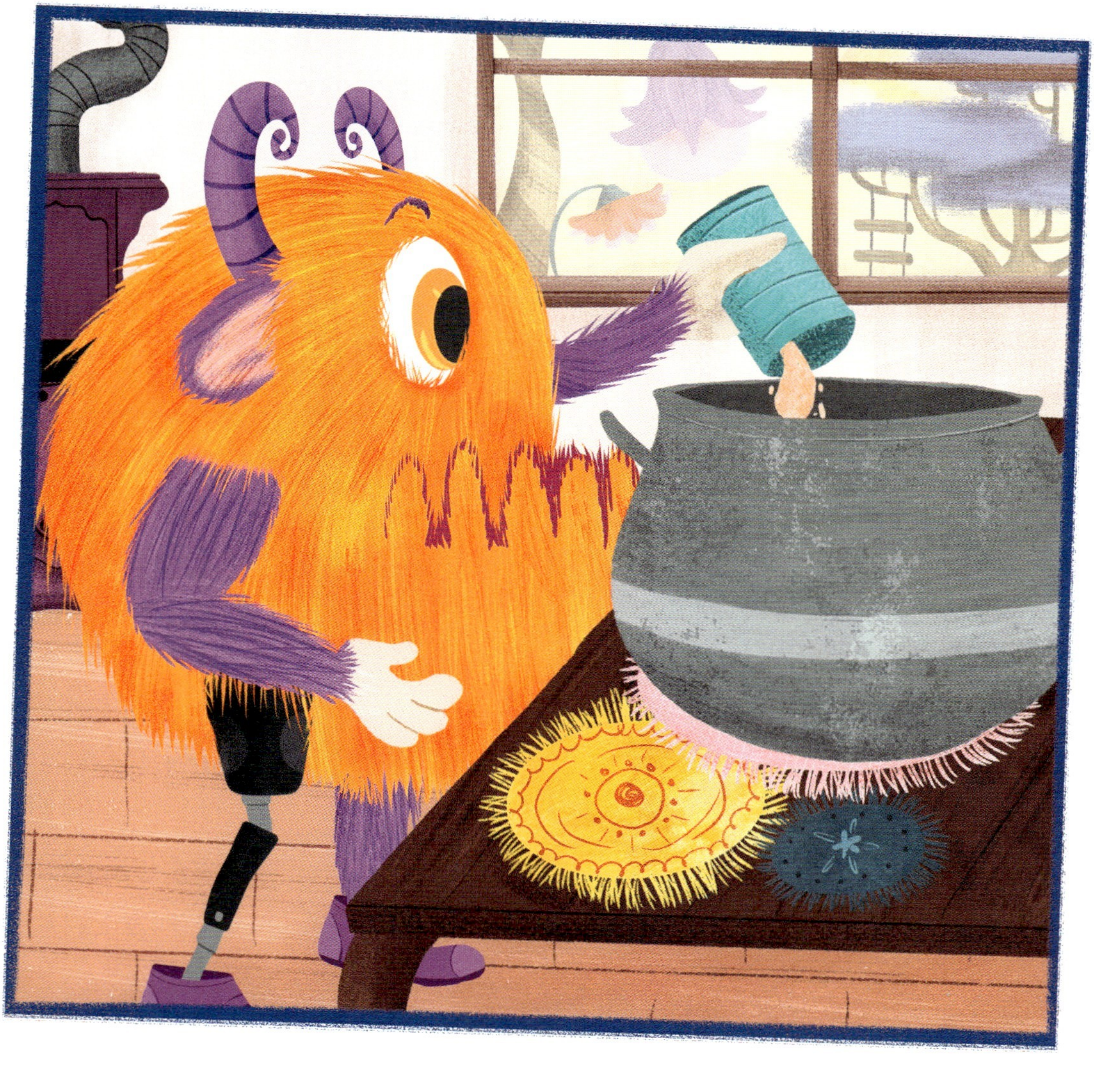

Tad tips in a tin.

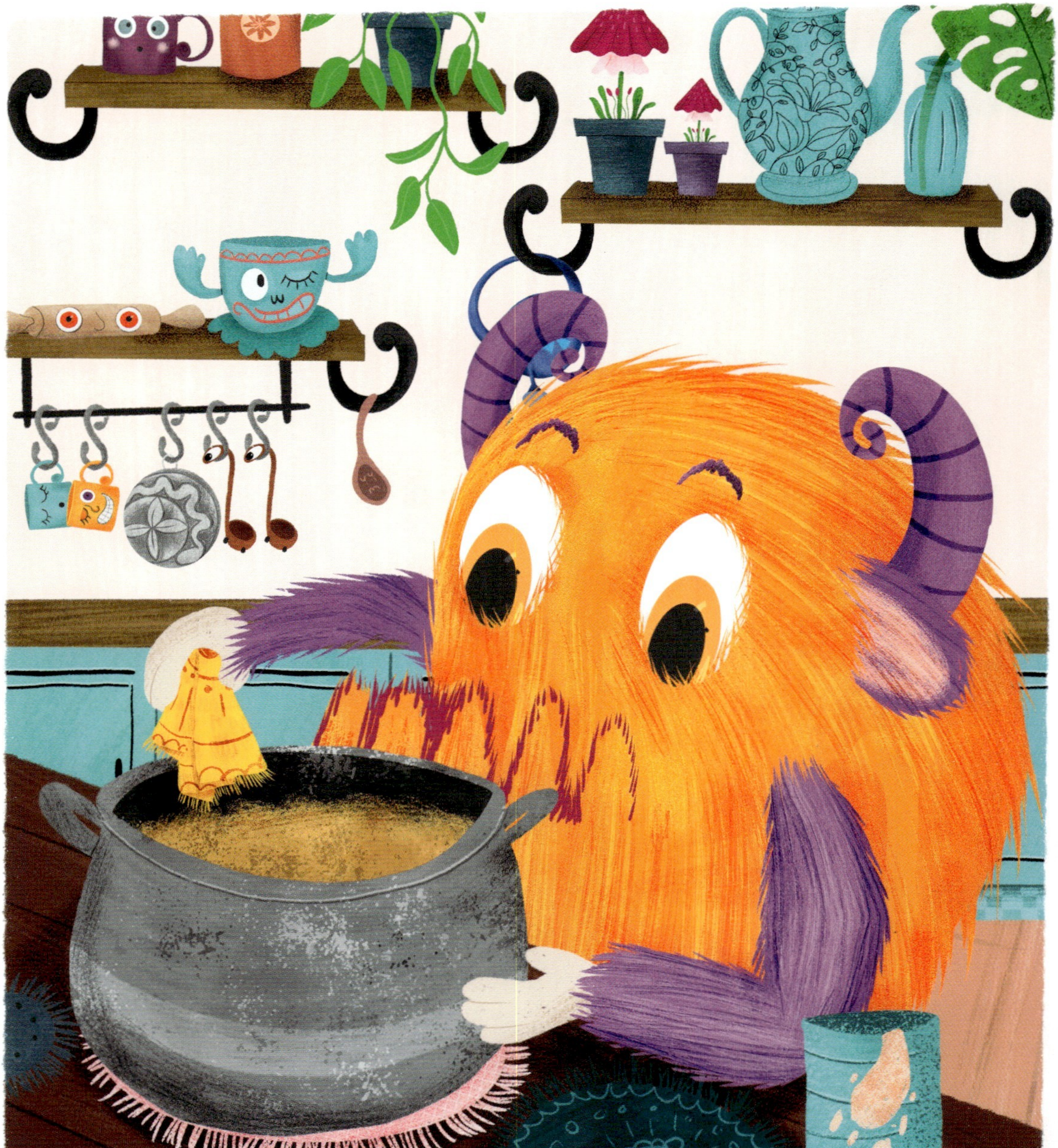

Tad dips in a mat.

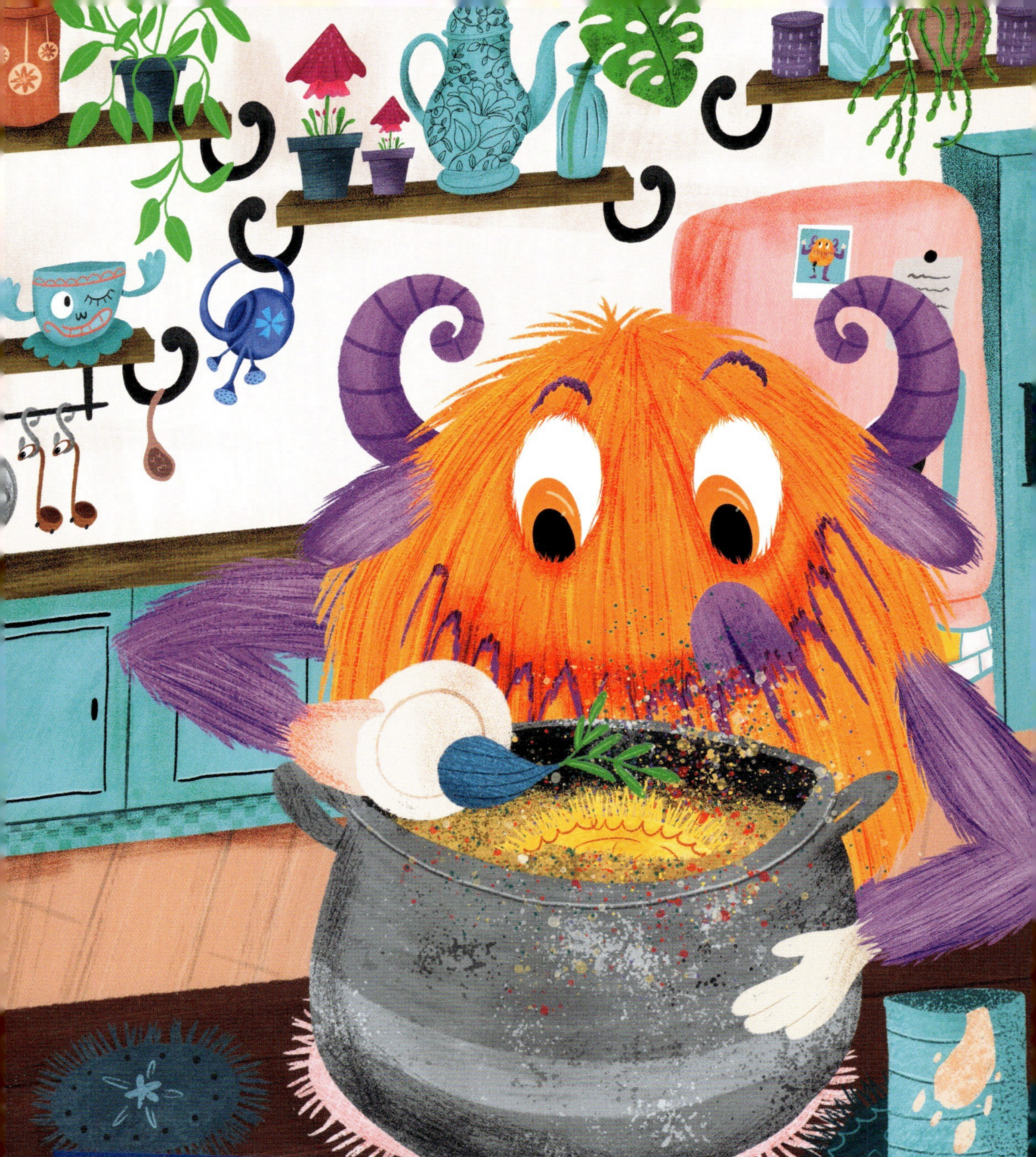

Tad tips in a pip.

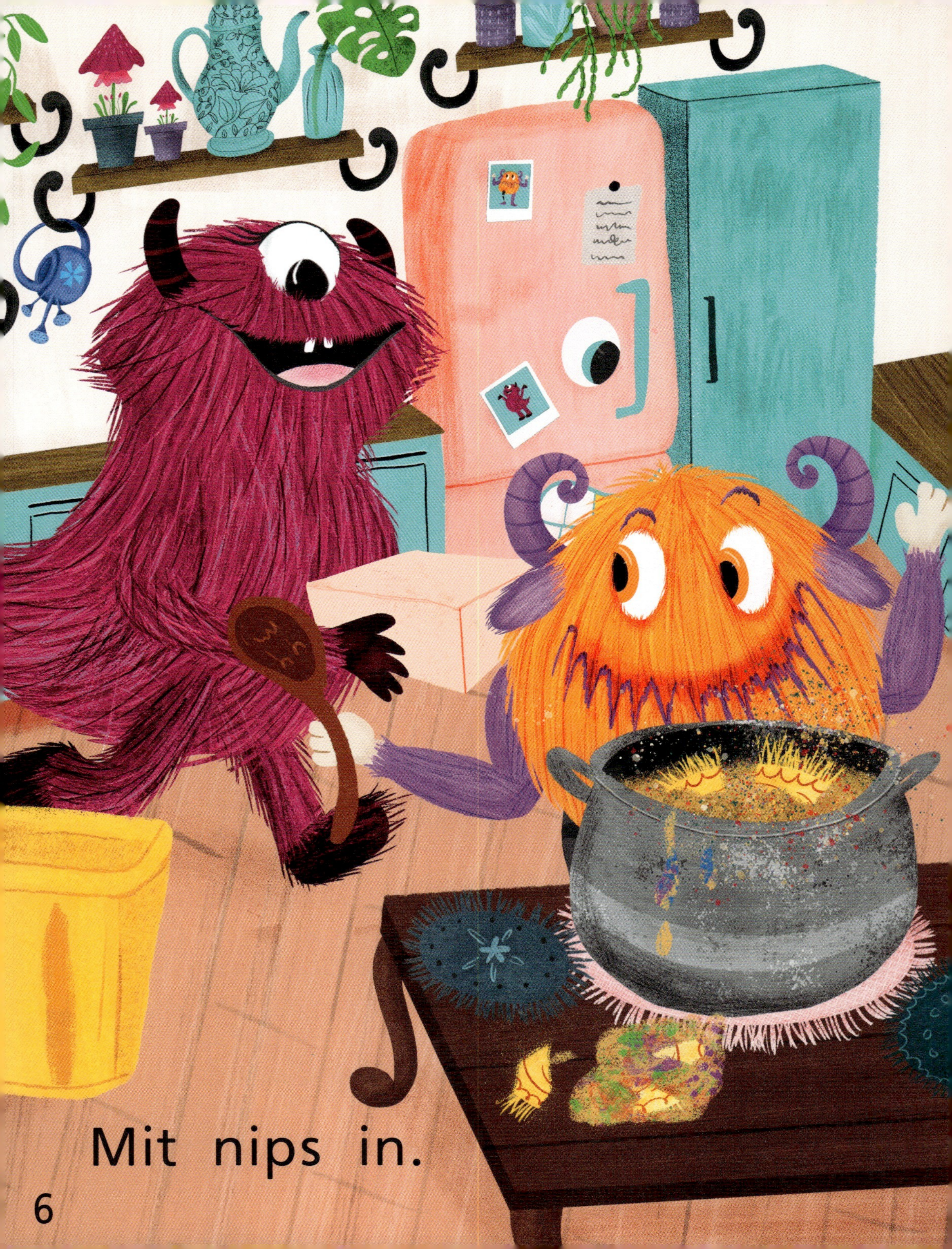

Mit nips in.

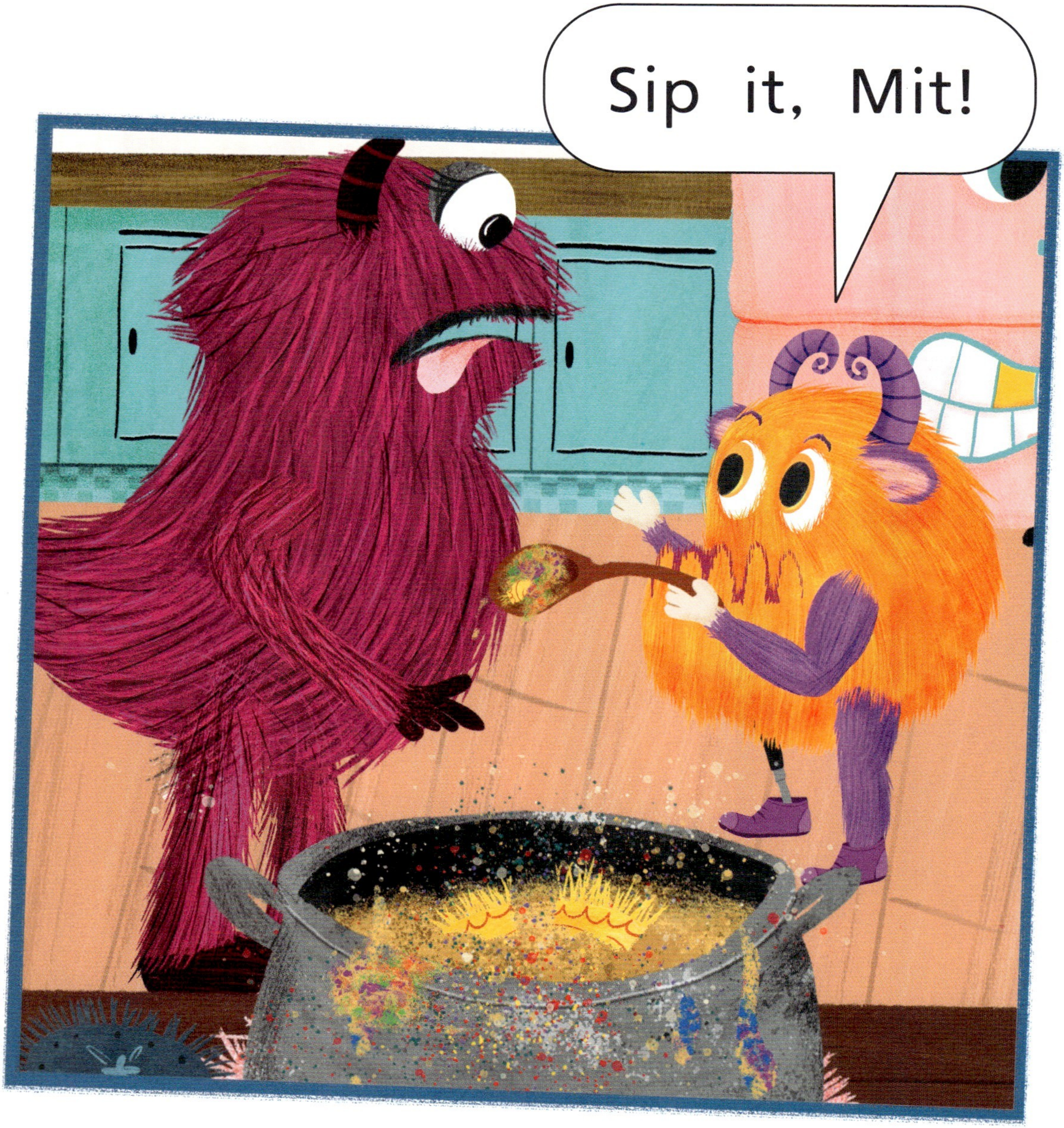
Sip it, Mit!

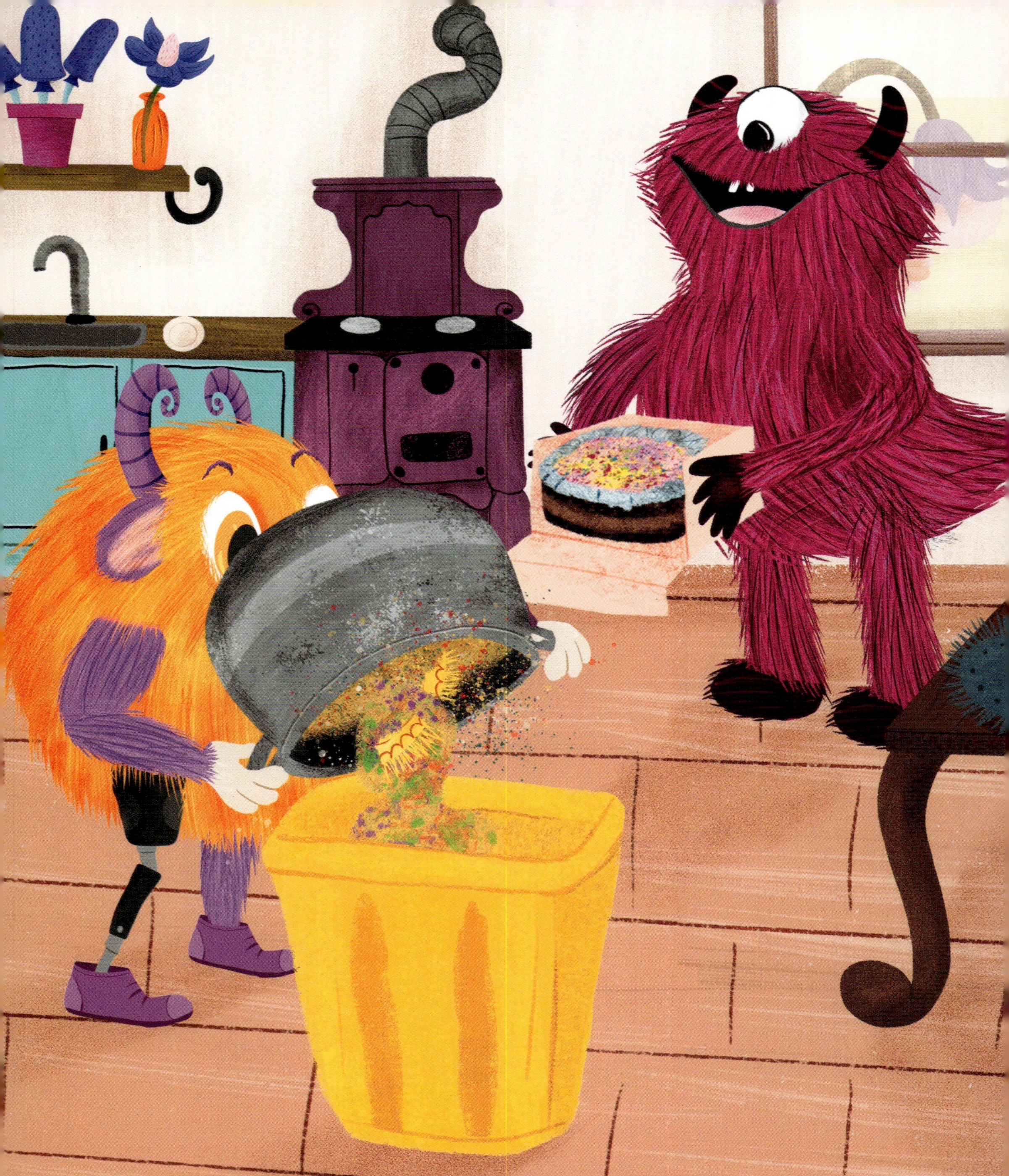

Tad tips it!